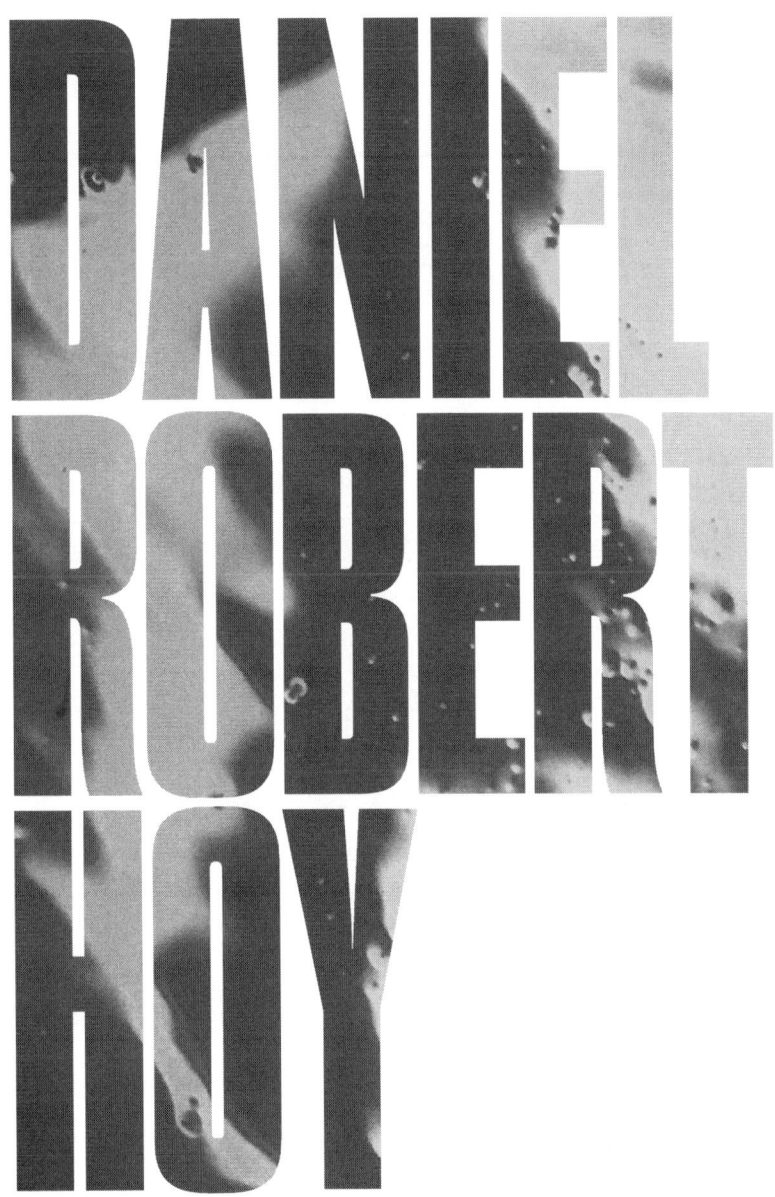

DANIEL ROBERT HOY

Tabletop Book, *MMXVIII*

Daniel Robert Hoy
Thought Provoking
Poetically Very Short Stories
Written by *Daniel Robert Hoy*
Wrote Daily (05/04/17 THRU 05/03/18)

Each story is a combination of Hemingway's *Shortest Story Ever* and a feeling at times of a haiku.

THANK YOU TO

MY FAMILY AND

FRIENDS FOR ALL

THEIR SUPPORT !

ISBN 978-1-09836-380-2

BLUE SKY !
ANGELS DIVE !
SUCCESSFUL RESCUE !

Written by Daniel Robert Hoy
on 05/04/17

UNVEILS PEDDLES !
HOPE ARRIVES !
APRIL SNOWDEVIL !

Written by Daniel Robert Hoy
on 05/05/17

GREEN BULLY !
BULLY BULLY !
GREEN GREEN !

Written by Daniel Robert Hoy
on 05/06/17

GLOWING ERUPTION !
HALTING GLASS !
THICKNESS ENSUES !

Written by Daniel Robert Hoy
on 05/07/17

WATER RUNS !
EVAPORATION ACCELERATES !
LONELY WORLD !

Written by Daniel Robert Hoy
on 05/08/17

CONSTANT SIGNAL !
SPINE PULSES !
CHANGE RELIEF !

Written by Daniel Robert Hoy
on 05/09/17

WORDS ANEW !
WAR ENSUES !
COMMUNICATION BEGINS !

Written by Daniel Robert Hoy
On 05/10/17

SILENT BEAUTY !
STORY WITHIN !
FREED THINKER !

Written by Daniel Robert Hoy
on 05/11/17

DECEPTIVE TRADE-POST !
MILLENNIAL SPIES !
BOTH NEEDED !

Written by Daniel Robert Hoy
On 05/12/17

OPEN DOOR !
LIGHT SHINES !
OUTAGE ENTERS !

Written by Daniel Robert Hoy
on 05/13/17

DRONE WAR !
WATER PLUGS !
FLIPPED TRAINS !

Written by Daniel Robert Hoy
on 05/14/17

HORIZON EXPANDS !
MARCHING LOUDLY !
BIRDS ENGAGED !

Written by Daniel Robert Hoy
on 05/15/17

PENCIL MARKS !
FINGER SCROLLS !
VANISHING VIEW !

Written by Daniel Robert Hoy
on 05/16/17

GODS GIFT !
SOCIETY REMOVES !
GIFT OPENED !

Written by Daniel Robert Hoy
on 05/17/17

HEARING BREATH !
FILTERS THROUGH !
RHYTHM FLOWING !

Written by Daniel Robert Hoy
on 05/18/17

WEAR WORDS !
NOT SORRY !
BE YOU !

Written by Daniel Robert Hoy
on 05/07/17

NO TECH !
TECH KNOW !
NOW THINK !

Written by Daniel Robert Hoy
on 05/20/17

SHOVEL FILLED !
SOIL DUMPED !
HEAVENLY GROUNDED !

Written by Daniel Robert Hoy
on 05/21/17

EYES WALTZING !
CROWD LONGING !
SHIP WRECKED !

Written by Daniel Robert Hoy
on 05/22/17

CENTER PERSEVERES !
BLADES CIRCLING !
SPRAWLING MESSAGES !

Written by Daniel Robert Hoy
on 05/23/17

EXPANSION INTERNALLY !
MOVING WILLINGLY !
OUTSIDE FILTERED !

Written by Daniel Robert Hoy
on 05/24/17

MUSCLES BURNING !
MOTIONLESS BODY !
REFUELING COMPLETE !

Written by Daniel Robert Hoy
on 05/25/17

CAPTIVATED THINKING !
SCROLLING UP !
REASONING SUPPRESSED !

Written by Daniel Robert Hoy
on 05/26/17

FEELING FOCUSED !
ADJUSTED TARGET !
ENJOYED TODAY !

Written by Daniel Robert Hoy
on 05/27/17

INVADING DROPLETS !
SWEPT AWAY !
GATHERING FORCEFULLY !

Written by Daniel Robert Hoy
on 05/28/17

MAKING HISTORY !
WOOD GRAINS !
REFRESHING CIRCULATION !

Written by Daniel Robert Hoy
on 05/29/17

VIEWING OCEAN !
SKY INVADES !
LIGHT PROTECTS !

Written by Daniel Robert Hoy
on 05/30/17

CLEARLY MUD !
GOVERNED CONFUSION !
FEW BENEFITS !

Written by Daniel Robert Hoy
on 05/31/17

WALLED VISION !
COURSE TEXTURE !
SEARING BREAKTHROUGH !

Written by Daniel Robert Hoy
on 06/01/17

UNNECESSARY MATERIALS !
OVER ABUNDANCE !
CHRONOLOGICAL KILLER !

Written by Daniel Robert Hoy
on 06/02/17

PAPERLESS SURROUNDINGS !
UNPLUGGED WORLD !
PENCIL REQUIRED !

Written by Daniel Robert Hoy
on 06/03/17

NOISE FLIES !
DRUMS DISCONNECTED !
MISSED OPPORTUNITY !

Written by Daniel Robert Hoy
on 06/04/17

TAPED SHADOW !
BRIGHTLY OUTLINED !
SUNSET TRANSFORMS !

Written by Daniel Robert Hoy
on 06/05/17

EYELIDS CLOSED !
BREATH NUMBING !
SOUL ARRIVED !

Written by Daniel Robert Hoy
on 06/06/17

WASTING KNOWLEDGE !
KNEW WHO !
NO ONE !

Written by Daniel Robert Hoy
on 06/07/17

SOIL RICH !
STEMS TANGLED !
GRASPING PROTECTION !

Written by Daniel Robert Hoy
on 06/08/17

GOLDEN TOPPED !
SAPPHIRE LAMP !
SKYLINE REACHING !
Written by Daniel Robert Hoy
on 06/09/17

SHARP WORDS !
DULLY RECEIVED !
HEALED BOTH !
Written by Daniel Robert Hoy
on 06/10/17

MANY VIEWS !
WITHOUT FOCUS !
CATCHES COLORS !
Written by Daniel Robert Hoy
on 06/11/17

LINES NARROWING !
GRASPING WHEEL !
FUTURISTIC FOOTAGE !
Written by Daniel Robert Hoy
on 06/12/17

QUALITY REQUIRED !
BODY REFUELED !
RADIANT RESULTS !
Written by Daniel Robert Hoy
on 06/13/17

AWOKEN HUMAN !
STRETCHING UPRIGHT !
INTELLECTUALLY STARVING !
Written by Daniel Robert Hoy
on 06/14/17

SOUND RUNNING !
SEPARATING NOISE !
TRANSPARENTLY DESTINE !
Written by Daniel Robert Hoy
on 06/15/17

INNER PEACE !
OUTWARD AURA !
THANKFULNESS OVERTAKES !
Written by Daniel Robert Hoy
on 06/16/17

ARM CHAIRS !
SHOULDERS SHRUG !
BACK CRACKED !
Written by Daniel Robert Hoy
on 06/17/17

STARE PROLONGED !
REPLICATING FORM !
IMPRESSION ENHANCING !
Written by Daniel Robert Hoy
on 06/18/17

STACKED ASHES !
GLARING THROUGH !
MEMORIES CRACKLING !
Written by Daniel Robert Hoy
on 06/19/17

TENSION WIRED !
ELECTRIFIED HARMONY !
COMFORT RESONATES !
Written by Daniel Robert Hoy
on 06/20/17

ENERGY SOURCE !
HUMAN GENERATED !
MUSCLE BUILT !

Written by Daniel Robert Hoy
on 06/21/17

FAINT RECOLLECTION !
AMBULANCE REMEMBERED !
TEARS FLOW !

Written by Daniel Robert Hoy
on 06/22/17

CANVAS SAILS !
COLORS CHISELING !
COATINGS PROPELLED !

Written by Daniel Robert Hoy
on 06/23/17

SHOCKED WITNESS !
BATTLING JUSTICE !
COURT SETTLING !

Written by Daniel Robert Hoy
on 06/24/17

WHY COMPLY !
HEAL WORLD !
KIND MAN !

Written by Daniel Robert Hoy
on 06/25/17

SUNNY BONFIRE !
ROASTING CLOUDS !
THIRST QUENCHED !

Written by Daniel Robert Hoy
on 06/26/17

SHOES TOSSED !
BEARING WALK !
EARTH SHATTERING !

Written by Daniel Robert Hoy
on 06/27/17

LIVING PRESENTS !
AGELESS TIME !
WORLDLY WONDERFUL !

Written by Daniel Robert Hoy
on 06/28/17

EAGERLY EARNING !
GAINING GOODS !
DISPLAYED NOWHERE !

Written by Daniel Robert Hoy
on 06/29/17

REFLECTION REQUIRED !
EVERYONES GIFTED !
COGNIZANT FEW !

Written by Daniel Robert Hoy
on 06/30/17

RAISING BEGAN !
NURTURED MIDDLE !
BEAUTIFUL ENDING !

Written by Daniel Robert Hoy
on 07/01/17

COMPREHENSION IGNORED !
CONFORMED MINDSET !
BEGRUDGED BACKING !

Written by Daniel Robert Hoy
on 07/02/17

SYMMETRICAL FOLIAGE !
BURLY BREEZES !
DIRECTIONALLY BENDING !

Written by Daniel Robert Hoy
on 07/03/17

DEEPENING RHYTHMS !
OCCASIONAL RESTFULNESS !
DYNAMIC BEATS !

Written by Daniel Robert Hoy
on 07/04/17

ORGANS PERFORMING !
REPLENISHED NUTRIENTS !
SOULFUL HYDRATION !

Written by Daniel Robert Hoy
on 07/05/17

DETERMINED ADRENALINE !
SILENCING MIND !
INTELLECTUALLY ACCOMPLISHED !

Written by Daniel Robert Hoy
on 07/06/17

SWEET SMELLS !
SUSPENDED SCENT !
SURROUNDING SATISFACTION !

Written by Daniel Robert Hoy
on 07/07/17

ASSEMBLED STRAIGHTAWAY !
CLASHING UNBROKEN !
EVERYBODY NEVERMORE !

Written by Daniel Robert Hoy
on 07/08/17

HIGH RIDER !
WHEELS ROLLING !
CIRCLING EARTH !

Written by Daniel Robert Hoy
on 07/09/17

ASCENDING SAUNTER !
FORTRESS MOBILIZED !
WAGING WARFARE !

Written by Daniel Robert Hoy
on 07/10/17

PLANK PROMENADES !
DANCING DAGGERS !
NOSEDIVE PLUNGE !

Written by Daniel Robert Hoy
on 07/11/17

MOUNTAINEERING DOGTROT !
CORPSE UNEARTHED !
MAYOR SUSPICION !

Written by Daniel Robert Hoy
on 07/12/17

METHODICAL MORNING !
YONDER INVASION !
SHIELD PLANET !

Written by Daniel Robert Hoy
on 07/13/17

PIDDLING UNDERACHIEVER !
ADVOCATES ENTICED !
RESPECTFULLY STARTLED !

Written by Daniel Robert Hoy
on 07/14/17

ENGULFED WILDFIRE !
DROWNING CRACKLE !
ESCAPE ALLOTTED !

Written by Daniel Robert Hoy
on 07/15/17

SUNRISING DOUGHNUTS !
MAYDAYS BOTTLENECKING !
BURDENED BELLYFUL !

Written by Daniel Robert Hoy
on 07/16/17

PARACHUTING OFFSHOOTS !
PLANECRASHED OASIS !
LIFEBOAT EMANCIPATION !

Written by Daniel Robert Hoy
on 07/17/17

BARELY SIGHTSEEING !
STARING GRIZZLY !
HONEYCOMB DRIZZLING !

Written by Daniel Robert Hoy
on 07/18/17

PETRIFIED FEAT !
CALLOUSLY PRANCING !
INDIVIDUALITY BEGINS !

Written by Daniel Robert Hoy
on 07/19/17

TREASURE PEGGED !
PATCHING LEG !
EYED CHEST !

Written by Daniel Robert Hoy
on 07/20/17

DISLOYAL AUTOMATION !
UPSETTING CREATION !
NABBED LIVING !

Written by Daniel Robert Hoy
on 07/21/17

CLAMBERING BARRIER !
PATHWAY PROBED !
PERCEIVED BORDERLINES !

Written by Daniel Robert Hoy
On 07/22/17

CAPERED CACHE !
LOOTING LUXURY !
OCCASIONALLY ENTITLED !

Written by Daniel Robert Hoy
on 07/23/17

HIGH WIRED !
SHAKING TENSION !
RISKY HESITATION !

Written by Daniel Robert Hoy
on 07/24/17

DESERT CRAWL !
HALLUCINATING OASIS !
EVAPORATED THIRST !

Written by Daniel Robert Hoy
on 07/25/17

BLINDING SUPERNOVA !
ANNIHILATING METEORITE !
ESCAPED INFINITY !

Written by Daniel Robert Hoy
on 07/26/17

PEDIGREE IMBEDDED !
ACCOMMODATING INERTIA !
CYNICAL INDOCTRINATION !

Written by Daniel Robert Hoy
on 07/27/17

LAUNCHING MARATHON !
ENDURING FRENZY !
INTERTWINED FINALE !

Written by Daniel Robert Hoy
on 07/28/17

ENCOMPASSING SAILS !
MAGNETIZED VORTEX !
GARNISH WINDS !

Written by Daniel Robert Hoy
on 07/29/17

STARVING SURVIVOR !
INTERVENES SHOOTS !
TARGETED FEAST !

Written by Daniel Robert Hoy
on 07/30/17

ROLLING ROCKS !
PRESSURED CRUSH !
SALTY PEPPER !

Written by Daniel Robert Hoy
on 07/31/17

AIRY MOUNTAINEERING !
EVADING AVALANCHE !
SAFELY RETURNED !

Written by Daniel Robert Hoy
on 08/01/17

TRIANGULATED MIRRORS !
EMULATING RUMINATION !
ERASES YORE !

Written by Daniel Robert Hoy
on 08/02/17

EYESIGHT ECHOES !
PUNGENT PALATE !
EXECUTION EMBRACED !

Written by Daniel Robert Hoy
on 08/03/17

TANGLED CAVERN !
FLUTTERING WALLS !
FLOORS SCREECHING !

Written by Daniel Robert Hoy
on 08/04/17

WAYWARD CRITTER !
NEIGHBORHOOD SEARCHING !
RESCUED ALIVE !

Written by Daniel Robert Hoy
on 08/05/17

MENTALLY STRONG !
SIMMERING COALS !
ATTAINED FEAT !

Written by Daniel Robert Hoy
on 08/06/17

PARACHUTING DROPLET !
NAVIGATED OCEANVIEW !
FOWL SOARS !

Written by Daniel Robert Hoy
on 08/07/17

RAGED LAVA !
VOLCANO ERUPTS !
ASHES PLUME !

Written by Daniel Robert Hoy
on 08/08/17

BLUE MOON !
MELLOWING MOMENT !
EPICALLY JUNCTURES !

Written by Daniel Robert Hoy
on 08/09/17

SWAYING WINDOW !
VACATED SPOT !
JOYOUS REMEMBRANCE !

Written by Daniel Robert Hoy
on 08/10/17

MYSTICALLY OVERLOOKED !
OBJECT FOUND !
SUSPECT WHO !

Written by Daniel Robert Hoy
on 08/11/17

STAGED PERFORMANCE !
SILENCING VOICES !
CAMOUFLAGES TRANSLATION !

Written by Daniel Robert Hoy
on 08/12/17

MAGNIFIED LEAP !
SKYROCKETING SPLASH !
LAKE DRAINED !

Written by Daniel Robert Hoy
on 08/13/17

PRAIRIES SKY !
BEAUTIFUL GRASSLANDS !
PLAINLY STANDSTILL !

Written by Daniel Robert Hoy
on 08/14/17

BLIZZARD BLINDNESS !
SNOWSHOEING DRUDGE !
ADVANCING AVALANCHE !

Written by Daniel Robert Hoy
on 08/15/17

SMELTING IRON !
LIMESTONE STACKED !
STOLEN CARBONATION !

Written by Daniel Robert Hoy
on 08/16/17

MURPHY'S JUSTICE !
HANGING BILL !
ORIGAMI CHAD !

Written by Daniel Robert Hoy
on 08/17/17

HORIZON PEOPLE !
PURPOSEFULLY SURROUNDS !
CITYSCAPE SHINES !

Written by Daniel Robert Hoy
on 08/18/17

SATURATED SANDS !
WAVES SHAPING !
BEACH BESTOWED !

Written by Daniel Robert Hoy
on 08/19/17

BROACHED VEGETATION !
CAPSTONES AFLOAT !
SCHEMINGLY SWAMPED !
Written by Daniel Robert Hoy
on 08/20/17

EMOTIONAL HEARTS !
FEELINGS BURST !
GIVING THANKS !
Written by Daniel Robert Hoy
on 08/21/17

BEHIND ECLIPSE !
POWERFUL SCENES !
FALLING AHEAD !
Written by Daniel Robert Hoy
on 08/22/17

TOWERING ANT !
EXCRUCIATING SECTIONS !
EARTHLY STOMPING !
Written by Daniel Robert Hoy
on 08/23/17

CORE CENTERPIECE !
LAYERING SPHERE !
INTERGALACTICALLY SPACED !
Written by Daniel Robert Hoy
on 08/24/17

DOMES SPINNING !
STATUES DANCING !
COLORFUL GOD !
Written by Daniel Robert Hoy
on 08/25/17

DETERMINED SOUL !
UNCREDITED STRENGTH !
TRACK ESTABLISHED !
Written by Daniel Robert Hoy
on 08/26/17

SAUNTERING NIGHTFALLS !
RACKETY NOCTURNALS !
PROWLING LIGHTLESSNESS !
Written by Daniel Robert Hoy
on 08/27/17

CLAY KNEADED !
DEHYDRATING POTTERY !
INTOXICATED KILN !
Written by Daniel Robert Hoy
on 08/28/17

FORKED RIVER !
RIPPLING SPOONFUL !
NATURALLY SLICED !
Written by Daniel Robert Hoy
on 08/29/17

PIERCING LOCOMOTIVE !
DAM DISMANTLED !
RAILING WHIRLWINDS !
Written by Daniel Robert Hoy
on 08/30/17

BRAZING METALS !
JOINTLY MELTED !
FILLING STRONG !
Written by Daniel Robert Hoy
on 08/31/17

MESHED MONOMERS !
SHACKLING POLYMERS !
PRODUCTIVELY POLYMERIZATION !

Written by Daniel Robert Hoy
on 09/01/17

CHILLING SUNSHINE !
RADIANTLY GLOWING !
CIVILIZED HEATWAVE !

Written by Daniel Robert Hoy
on 09/02/17

GRATIFYING GARBAGE !
QUALITY YEARNING !
WASTEFULLY BANISHED !

Written by Daniel Robert Hoy
on 09/03/17

BOILING SAP !
SUGAR SHACKED !
TAPPING MAPLE !

Written by Daniel Robert Hoy
on 09/04/17

SUBWOOFER BASS !
AMPLIFYING WATER !
ACOUSTICALLY SOUND !

Written by Daniel Robert Hoy
on 09/05/17

TWISTING STRANDS !
FIBERS BRAIDED !
SECURELY JUMPING !

Written by Daniel Robert Hoy
on 09/06/17

WHEELS GRINDING !
DULLY DRAGGING !
ABRASIVELY STONED !

Written by Daniel Robert Hoy
on 09/07/17

SCHEMINGLY GOVERNED !
MOVING PAWNS !
RUBBER STAMPED !

Written by Daniel Robert Hoy
on 09/08/17

EXTRUDING MAGMA !
FIERCELY EXPLODES !
THUNDERING PYRAMID !

Written by Daniel Robert Hoy
on 09/09/17

STEEL YOURSELF !
UNCOILED CYCLONE !
SCALING GATORS !

Written by Daniel Robert Hoy
on 09/10/17

HARVESTED SEEDS !
LIVESTOCKS FEEDING !
NURTURING FERTILIZERS !

Written by Daniel Robert Hoy
on 09/11/17

MAINTAINING CHARGE !
VOLTAGE WORKING !
ELECTRIFYING ENERGY !

Written by Daniel Robert Hoy
on 09/12/17

GAUGED JOURNEYMEN !
MACHINING CAPABILITIES !
CASTINGS TOOLS !
Written by Daniel Robert Hoy
on 09/13/17

HEATED RESINS !
MOLDS ROTATING !
UNSHAKABLY DESIGNED !
Written by Daniel Robert Hoy
on 09/14/17

CRUSHED STONES !
FURNACE COOKING !
LIQUEFYING STEEL !
Written by Daniel Robert Hoy
on 09/15/17

ROLLING CONVEYOR !
TRUCKS ASSEMBLED !
LOGISTICALLY ENGINEERED !
Written by Daniel Robert Hoy
on 09/16/17

PRACTICALLY NUTS !
BOLTING DETAILS !
SPECIFICALLY FASTENED !
Written by Daniel Robert Hoy
on 09/17/17

HAMMERING POINTS !
WORDSMITHS FORGING !
BOWING REMARKS !
Written by Daniel Robert Hoy
on 09/18/17

JURY INJECTION !
TOLERATING JUDGEMENT !
LEGALLY BINDING !
Written by Daniel Robert Hoy
on 09/19/17

SPINNERS HEIGHTENED !
PROPELLING UPROAR !
LAUNCHED HOSTILITY !
Written by Daniel Robert Hoy
on 09/20/17

HOLLOWED BRAINS !
MOLDS HEADLINED !
CASTING ENLIGHTENMENT !
Written by Daniel Robert Hoy
on 09/21/17

STARVING SKELETON !
MELTING DESIRE !
REKINDLING PERSONAGE !
Written by Daniel Robert Hoy
on 09/22/17

INDOCTRINATED TUBES !
FLOWING RELIGION !
DEFLECTING SANCTITY !
Written by Daniel Robert Hoy
on 09/23/17

MILLING SHAPES !
DRILLED IMPRESSIONS !
METALLICALLY DISPLAYED !
Written by Daniel Robert Hoy
on 09/24/17

UPLIFTING OUTDOORS !
TECHNOLOGY DEPRESSED !
EXTERNALIZED INTERNALLY !

Written by Daniel Robert Hoy
on 09/25/17

PROTECTING COSMOS !
LAMINATED LANDSCAPING !
ACCENTUATING VIEW !

Written by Daniel Robert Hoy
on 09/26/17

PROGRAMMED TACTICS !
COMBATING NUMERICALLY !
AXIS DIVERTING !

Written by Daniel Robert Hoy
on 09/27/17

TOWERING BROADCAST !
INDEPENDENCE COMMUNICATED !
EMBRACING CULTURE !

Written by Daniel Robert Hoy
on 09/28/17

ACTUATED SELF !
SCULPTURING UNIQUENESS !
FREEDOM DELIVERED !

Written by Daniel Robert Hoy
on 09/29/17

HANDLING ATOMS !
MOLECULES CHAINED !
COMPOUNDS LATCHING !

Written by Daniel Robert Hoy
on 09/30/17

CLENCHED KITES !
LEVERAGING BUBBLES !
BALLOONS CATAPULTING !

Written by Daniel Robert Hoy
on 10/01/17

PERFORATED CRYSTALS !
BARGING MESH !
GLACIERS HOVERING !

Written by Daniel Robert Hoy
on 10/02/17

WIRED LIFELINE !
EMPOWERING CONDUCTIVITY !
AIRING ORE !

Written by Daniel Robert Hoy
on 10/03/17

CHAIRED HORIZON !
TABLING PLATEAU !
BEDROCK DOZING !

Written by Daniel Robert Hoy
on 10/04/17

VALUED WORKMANSHIP !
STRENGTHENING JOINTS !
CRAFTSMANSHIPS REVIVAL !

Written by Daniel Robert Hoy
on 10/05/17

AGING GRAINS !
TIMBERED LUXURIES !
ROOTS AWAKENING !

Written by Daniel Robert Hoy
on 10/06/17

TRIPLES BUNKED !
DOUBLING TRUNDLES !
LOFTY ONES !

Written by Daniel Robert Hoy
on 10/07/17

TWIGS BUDDING !
BRANCHES RAILED !
TRUNKS AFLOAT !

Written by Daniel Robert Hoy
on 10/08/17

SIMPLY DESIGNED !
CHAIRED MISSION !
WOVEN SEATS !

Written by Daniel Robert Hoy
on 10/09/17

ROLLING CONVEYOR !
TRUCKS ASSEMBLED !
LOGISTICALLY ENGINEERED !

Written by Daniel Robert Hoy
on 09/16/17

PRACTICALLY NUTS !
BOLTING DETAILS !
SPECIFICALLY FASTENED !

Written by Daniel Robert Hoy
on 09/17/17

HAMMERING POINTS !
WORDSMITHS FORGING !
BOWING REMARKS !

Written by Daniel Robert Hoy
on 09/18/17

UNHINGED HOPES !
TAINTING CHEST !
BURIED TREASURES !

Written by Daniel Robert Hoy

TREES PARADING !
MARCHING HIGHER !
TIMBERLINE EVAPORATING !

Written by Daniel Robert Hoy

BAKED CRUST !
STEAMING FILLING !
SMELLING PIES !

Written by Daniel Robert Hoy

PROTECTING WARES !
RUGGEDLY SOFT !
SCENTED LEATHERS !

Written by Daniel Robert Hoy
on 10/13/17

BRIMMED HAT !
MOUNTING HORSE !
REINING WORLDWIDE !

Written by Daniel Robert Hoy
on 10/14/17

FLAGGED NOMENCLATURES !
SHIPPING MERCHANDISE !
ECONOMIZING CONVENIENCE !

Written by Daniel Robert Hoy
on 10/15/17

WHISTLING BRASS !
CORK ENCLOSED !
MUSICALLY REFEREED !

Written by Daniel Robert Hoy
on 10/16/17

BAPTIZED CLAY !
SURRENDERING WHEEL !
KILNED CHALICE !

Written by Daniel Robert Hoy
on 10/17/17

FLOATING TILES !
WALLED REALITY !
VIRTUALLY FLOORED !

Written by Daniel Robert Hoy
on 10/18/17

FORETELLING KEEPSAKES !
RELIVED ORIGINS !
FLASHBACKS RENOVATED !

Written by Daniel Robert Hoy
on 10/19/17

BRAIDED ANCESTORS !
WAVING HEIRLOOMS !
DESCENDANTS ENCIRCLING !

Written by Daniel Robert Hoy
on 10/20/17

UNERRING COUNTRYSIDE !
UNDISPUTED CITYSCAPE !
CULTURES CRYSTALLIZED !

Written by Daniel Robert Hoy
on 10/21/17

BUBBLING GLASS !
PIPER BLOWING !
BLOWPIPER GLASSBLOWING !

Written by Daniel Robert Hoy
on 10/22/17

STAINED GLASS !
HIGHLIGHTED PRAISE !
DELIBERATING GLOW !

Written by Daniel Robert Hoy
on 10/23/17

PREDICTING ISMS !
ANTIQUATED ORIGINAL !
PAINTED TRUTH !

Written by Daniel Robert Hoy
on 10/24/17

DIVINE DINING !
DESERVING DESSERT !
DELIGHTED DIALECT !

Written by Daniel Robert Hoy
on 10/25/17

ESTEEMED EGG !
SHELTERING COERCION !
SITTING DUCK !

Written by Daniel Robert Hoy
on 10/26/17

OPENED SCROLL !
CHASING WORDS !
LASTING CONQUEST !

Written by Daniel Robert Hoy
on 10/27/17

FETCHED TARGETS !
BARKING ACHIEVEMENTS !
OBJECTIVE SITTING !

Written by Daniel Robert Hoy
on 10/28/17

STRIKING PITCH !
SOUND DRUMMING !
BEATING HEARTS !

Written by Daniel Robert Hoy
on 10/29/17

CASTED IMAGE !
SCULPTURING PEACE !
FEARLESSLY FREED !

Written by Daniel Robert Hoy
on 10/30/17

CAGED HANDWRITING !
COMPOSING LIMITS !
CHOPPED CREATION !

Written by Daniel Robert Hoy
on 10/31/17

BARN LIVING !
STACKING HAY !
QUILTED WARMTH !

Written by Daniel Robert Hoy
on 11/01/17

WALKING STICKS !
STRIDES LONGING !
CATCHING FOOTSTEPS !

Written by Daniel Robert Hoy
on 11/02/17

HANDLING PAINTBRUSH !
BRISTLES SATURATED !
RIPPLING STROKES !

Written by Daniel Robert Hoy
on 11/03/17

EXERTING NOTABLE !
BOUNTIFULLY FLYING !
SOFTLY LANDED !

Written by Daniel Robert Hoy
on 11/04/17

POPULATION GROWING !
BEARING HABITATS !
VANISHED SPACE !

Written by Daniel Robert Hoy
on 11/05/17

PRIED WISDOM !
LEVERAGING KNOWLEDGE !
VIEW TORQUED !

Written by Daniel Robert Hoy
on 11/06/17

IMMERSING CLEANLINESS !
BRUSHING SURFACE !
SCRUBBED IMPURITIES !

Written by Daniel Robert Hoy
on 11/07/17

RAILING TASTEBUDS !
SURROUNDING CUISINES !
FORKED BARRIERS !

Written by Daniel Robert Hoy
on 11/08/17

MAINTAINING TOOLS !
FIXING WHATCHAMACALLIT !
TASK ACHIEVED !

Written by Daniel Robert Hoy
on 11/09/17

FLOATING ICE !
WATER FREEZING !
BITING CHILL !

Written by Daniel Robert Hoy
on 11/10/17

LOGGING CIRCLES !
STACKED SQUARES !
TRIANGLES PEAKING !

Written by Daniel Robert Hoy
on 11/11/17

INGREDIENTS FARMED !
MAKING RECIPES !
TASTEFULLY DINING !

Written by Daniel Robert Hoy
on 11/12/17

JOLTING COMPLAINTS !
UNCONTROLLED BICKERING !
JERKY BEEFED !

Written by Daniel Robert Hoy
on 11/13/17

DOORS PERMEATING !
BELONGINGS FLOORED !
PROLIFERATING STAIRWAY !

Written by Daniel Robert Hoy
on 11/14/17

LID REMOVED !
RETRIEVING COMFORT !
JAR EMPTIED !

Written by Daniel Robert Hoy
on 11/15/17

ROTATING WATERWHEELS !
EMPOWERING GEARS !
HYDROPOWER MILLED !

Written by Daniel Robert Hoy
on 11/16/17

MANEUVERING SOLUTIONS !
INNOVATIONS BROODING !
FIXATION SIMPLIFIED !

Written by Daniel Robert Hoy
on 11/17/17

BORING HOLE !
ROTATED BIT !
HONING ABYSS !

Written by Daniel Robert Hoy
on 11/18/17

BREEDING ORIGINS !
GENERATION INTRODUCED !
SUCCEEDING CULMINATION !

Written by Daniel Robert Hoy
on 11/19/17

INDIVIDUALIZED FLYING !
BODIES SOARING !
HOVERING DESTINATION !

Written by Daniel Robert Hoy
on 11/20/17

ROTATING SPHERES !
FRICTION ROLLING !
BEARING DEMANDS !

Written by Daniel Robert Hoy
on 11/21/17

LAUNCHING MOONWALKERS !
SPACESHIPS LIFTING !
EXTRATERRESTRIALS BEAMING !

Written by Daniel Robert Hoy
on 11/22/17

ENERGY CONVERTED !
EXERTING FORCE !
ENGINES DESIGNED !

Written by Daniel Robert Hoy
on 11/23/17

WARMING CONFIDENCE !
RISING PEACE !
SOUL SOLIDIFIED !

Written by Daniel Robert Hoy
on 11/24/17

LUMBERJACKS HARVESTING !
ROLLED LOGS !
SKIDDING ROADS !

Written by Daniel Robert Hoy
on 11/25/17

TRAVELING EAST !
REVERSING SUN !
EARTH UNDONE !

Written by Daniel Robert Hoy
on 11/26/17

SPINNING THOUGHTS !
WHEELS ROTATED !
TREADS NEUTRALIZED !

Written by Daniel Robert Hoy
on 11/27/17

TIME CRUNCHED !
INTELLECTUALLY MOVING !
FILLING SPACE !

Written by Daniel Robert Hoy
on 11/28/17

SERVING PLATEFULS !
STARVED PORTIONS !
FEEDING FAMINE !

Written by Daniel Robert Hoy
on 11/29/17

ENERGY FLOATING !
COATED EMERGENCE !
GLARING APPARITION !

Written by Daniel Robert Hoy
on 11/30/17

EYELASHES LIFTED !
LOADING EYELIDS !
BAGS HANDLED !

Written by Daniel Robert Hoy
on 12/01/17

DAZZLING LIGHT !
STANDING STILL !
SKY REACHED !

Written by Daniel Robert Hoy
on 12/02/17

FLAGS FLYING !
COLORING CLOUDS !
BACKDROP TRANSPIRING !
Written by Daniel Robert Hoy
on 12/03/17

UPLIFTING EYESIGHT !
REACHING BATTLEFIELD !
SOULS SLAYING !
Written by Daniel Robert Hoy
on 12/04/17

CLEANSING RIVER !
SURFACE WASHED !
FILTERING DOWNSTREAM !
Written by Daniel Robert Hoy
on 12/05/17

WARMING CONFIDENCE !
RISING PEACE !
SOUL SOLIDIFIED !
Written by Daniel Robert Hoy
on 11/24/17

LUMBERJACKS HARVESTING !
ROLLED LOGS !
SKIDDING ROADS !
Written by Daniel Robert Hoy
on 11/25/17

TRAVELING EAST !
REVERSING SUN !
EARTH UNDONE !
Written by Daniel Robert Hoy
on 11/26/17

TRACTOR CULTIVATING !
PLOWING FIELDS !
SOIL TILLED !
Written by Daniel Robert Hoy
on 12/06/17

PAINTED WALLS !
CHANGING COLORS !
MOODS EXPRESSED !
Written by Daniel Robert Hoy
on 12/07/17

GOVERNING PERFORMANCE !
ARRANGEMENT ELECTRIFYING !
SUPPLYING DEMAND !
Written by Daniel Robert Hoy
on 12/08/17

METAL HEATED !
HAMMERING SHAPE !
PART FORGED !
Written by Daniel Robert Hoy
on 12/09/17

AIRED DEW !
FOGGING VAPOR !
DROPLETS SUSPENDED !
Written by Daniel Robert Hoy
on 12/10/17

CYLINDER SHARPENED !
SCRAPING CONE !
CIRCLE SHAPED !
Written by Daniel Robert Hoy
on 12/11/17

OPERATING ROOM !
PERFORMING SURGERY !
TREATING CONDITION !

Written by Daniel Robert Hoy
on 12/12/17

CLAY PIPING !
MOVING WASTE !
ENVIRONMENTAL BREATHING !

Written by Daniel Robert Hoy
on 12/13/17

FIBER HARVESTED !
NATURE BONDING !
COMFORTING STRENGTH !

Written by Daniel Robert Hoy
on 12/14/17

GAS DISPERSED !
TRAPPING SPACES !
FOAM BUBBLING !

Written by Daniel Robert Hoy
on 12/15/17

BRAKING LIGHTS !
TRAFFIC CRAWLING !
ROADS THROTTLED !

Written by Daniel Robert Hoy
on 12/16/17

SKILLED DEPARTURE !
TEMPERAMENT FLYING !
STUMBLING ARRIVAL !

Written by Daniel Robert Hoy
on 12/17/17

BORDERS HINGING !
CONNECTING LANDS !
FIELDS OSCILLATING !

Written by Daniel Robert Hoy
on 12/18/17

CARRYING SOUND !
INFORMATION EXTRACTED !
TRANSFORMING ORIGINAL !

Written by Daniel Robert Hoy
on 12/19/17

STYLUS WRITING !
INSCRIBING TABLETS !
CLAY RETAINING !

Written by Daniel Robert Hoy
on 12/20/17

GIFT STRESSING !
TRAVELING AFAR !
SOUL HOLLOWED !

Written by Daniel Robert Hoy
on 12/21/17

DESERTED MOUNTAINTOP !
FREEZING SANDS !
AVALANCHE BEACHED !

Written by Daniel Robert Hoy
on 12/22/17

SPRINGING LAUNCH !
TOP REACHED !
ENERGIZING GRAVITATION !

Written by Daniel Robert Hoy
on 12/23/17

POWERBOATS PLANING !
PASSING PORTSIDE !
BOATERS WAVING !

Written by Daniel Robert Hoy
on 12/24/17

ROOF TOPPED !
WEARING CROWN !
PEAK REDEEMED !

Written by Daniel Robert Hoy
on 12/25/17

SNOW MASKING !
FOREST SILENCED !
PIERCING SHIVERS !

Written by Daniel Robert Hoy
on 12/26/17

JET STREAMING !
WINDS ENCIRCLED !
PROPELLING FLIGHT !

Written by Daniel Robert Hoy
on 12/27/17

PEARLS PLUNDERED !
PETRIFYING PITFALL !
PIRATES PERISHED !

Written by Daniel Robert Hoy
on 12/28/17

TRAVELLER EXPLORING !
ENCOMPASSING LANDMARK !
ERA DISCOVERED !

Written by Daniel Robert Hoy
on 12/29/17

HARP ENCHANTING !
ILLUMINATING HARDWOOD !
BAKER GAMBOLLING !

Written by Daniel Robert Hoy
on 12/30/17

HARNESSING COURAGE !
CAVALRY RIDING !
CONQUERING HOMELAND !

Written by Daniel Robert Hoy
on 12/31/17

FLIPPING HOURGLASS !
TIMEKEEPER POINTING !
BEGINNING QUEST !

Written by Daniel Robert Hoy
on 01/01/18

NERO SUCCUMBED !
LAKE FILLED !
COLOSSEUM ERECTED !

Written by Daniel Robert Hoy
on 01/02/18

DISTINGUISHED PALACE !
MARBLE CROWNING !
COMMEMORATING EMPRESS !

Written by Daniel Robert Hoy
on 01/03/18

SOUL MUMMIFIED !
RISING PYRAMID !
AFTERLIFE ETERNALIZED !

Written by Daniel Robert Hoy
on 01/04/18

CLIMBING WATCHTOWERS !
TORCHING SIGNALS !
DEFENDING WALL !

Written by Daniel Robert Hoy
on 01/05/18

SOUNDING TECTONIC !
EARTHQUAKE TRENCHING !
AMPLIFYING SEABED !

Written by Daniel Robert Hoy
on 01/06/18

GLOBALIZING FREEDOM !
FEEDING YOURSELF !
LIBERATING FARMING !

Written by Daniel Robert Hoy
on 01/07/18

INVADING SCHISMATIC !
EMPIRE SURRENDERED !
SPLITTING BELIEFS !

Written by Daniel Robert Hoy
on 01/08/18

FACING EARTH !
MOON PULLING !
RISING TIDE !

Written by Daniel Robert Hoy
on 01/09/18

NEURONS PITCHING !
PERFORMING BRAINWAVES !
FREQUENCIES HARMONIZING !

Written by Daniel Robert Hoy
on 01/10/18

WHISTLING BREEZE !
BREATH CHILLING !
GHOSTWRITING CLOUDS !

Written by Daniel Robert Hoy
on 01/11/18

DOCTOR FATIGUED !
EXHAUSTING SURGERIES !
MISPLACED ORGAN !

Written by Daniel Robert Hoy
on 01/12/18

STORMING COURTROOM !
LAWYER BLINDED !
UNSETTLING CASE !

Written by Daniel Robert Hoy
on 01/13/18

PUZZLING ACCOUNTANT !
MISSING NUMBERS !
FILED AWAY !

Written by Daniel Robert Hoy
on 01/14/18

LINKING STRUCTURES !
ENGINEER SWEATING !
GRASPING DETAILS !

Written by Daniel Robert Hoy
on 01/15/18

ENTREPRENEUR CREATING !
ANTICIPATED NEEDS !
REWARDING RISK !

Written by Daniel Robert Hoy
on 01/16/18

INTERRUPTING CELLPHONES !
FACES TALKING !
PERSONALIZING RELATIONSHIPS !

Written by Daniel Robert Hoy
on 01/17/18

ROASTING GARLIC !
TRANQUILIZING AROMA !
DINNER PERMEATING !

Written by Daniel Robert Hoy
on 01/18/18

SAVORING MUSHROOMS !
CARAMELIZED ONIONS !
TASTING BROCCOLI !

Written by Daniel Robert Hoy
on 01/19/18

CHERISHING NATURE !
PICKING APPLES!
THROWING STONES !

Written by Daniel Robert Hoy
on 01/20/18

HEARING WATERFALLS !
WIND HOWLING !
SPLASHING STEPS !

Written by Daniel Robert Hoy
on 01/21/18

VENTING VOLCANO !
WORLD ERUPTING !
OUTPOURING LAVA !

Written by Daniel Robert Hoy
on 01/22/18

SURROUNDING ISLAND !
TEARDROPS ISOLATED !
SUBMERGING PANORAMA !

Written by Daniel Robert Hoy
on 01/23/18

ENCHANTING THUNDERSTORM !
PLATEAU SLANTING !
FILLING BUCKETS !

Written by Daniel Robert Hoy
on 01/24/18

ESCAPING SAHARA !
STAR SWELTERING !
DESERTED SANDS !

Written by Daniel Robert Hoy
on 01/25/18

GREENGROCERIES REVIVED !
FREEING SEEDS !
PLETHORA PLANTED !

Written by Daniel Robert Hoy
on 01/26/18

RIPPLING RIVER !
PEBBLES SHINING !
REFLECTING SHORES !

Written by Daniel Robert Hoy
on 01/27/18

FLYING GRAVITY !
WINGS UNERRING !
UPLIFTING DESTINATION !

Written by Daniel Robert Hoy
on 01/28/18

OCEANS REACHING !
FLOATING LANDS !
DEEPENING BLUES !

Written by Daniel Robert Hoy
on 01/29/18

CAVEMEN HUNTING !
WHALES DOMINATING !
SEPARATING WORLDS !

Written by Daniel Robert Hoy
on 01/30/18

PREHISTORIC LIGHTNING !
CREATING FIRE !
HIPPOS SUBMERGING !

Written by Daniel Robert Hoy
on 01/31/18

OXEN PLOWING !
INTRODUCING AGRICULTURE !
SETTLING GATHERERS !

Written by Daniel Robert Hoy
on 02/01/18

FLATTENING CLAY !
TROJANS WRITING !
TRAVELING ODYSSEY !

Written by Daniel Robert Hoy
on 02/02/18

EMPIRE FALLING !
DRAGONS LASHING !
DARKENING SKIES !

Written by Daniel Robert Hoy
on 02/03/18

DISCOVERING EDGES !
CIRCLING GLOBE !
BEARS SURPRISING !

Written by Daniel Robert Hoy
on 02/04/18

FRENCH REVOLTING !
SLAUGHTERING PIGS !
FINE DINING !

Written by Daniel Robert Hoy
on 02/05/18

FULFILLING WELFARE !
MASTERED CLASSICS !
ENDLESSNESS TIMED !

Written by Daniel Robert Hoy
on 02/06/18

PRESENTING VIEW !
CONTEMPORARIES CONTRIBUTING !
JUDGING HENCEFORTH !

Written by Daniel Robert Hoy
on 02/07/18

RECHARGING CAPSULES !
ROBOTS MARCHING !
BATTLING SOUNDWAVES !

Written by Daniel Robert Hoy
on 02/08/18

UNDERGROUND GROWING !
FILTERED ENVIRONMENT !

Pods Launched !
Written by Daniel Robert Hoy
on 02/09/18

HUMANS CAPTURING !
ARRESTING HUMANOIDS !
CONTROLS RECYCLED !

Written by Daniel Robert Hoy
on 02/10/18

ZEUS CLONED !
DRONES CELEBRATING !
COERCING SUPERIORS !

Written by Daniel Robert Hoy
on 02/11/18

CELEBRATING CIRCUS !
WHALES SMOKING !
LIONS DRINKING !

Written by Daniel Robert Hoy
on 02/12/18

SMOKE CHOKING !
FIREFIGHTER RESCUING !
BABY SAVED !

Written by Daniel Robert Hoy
on 02/13/18

FILLING SPACE !
WORDS UNKNOWING !
UNSETTLING NERVES !

Written by Daniel Robert Hoy
on 02/14/18

ROOSTER CROWING !
EYES OPENED !
STARTING DAY !

Written by Daniel Robert Hoy
on 02/15/18

RISING STRETCH !
SHUTTERS OPENED !
DIRECTING SAIL !

Written by Daniel Robert Hoy
on 02/16/18

HOURS ORBITING !
IGNITING COFFEE !
SUNRISE LAUNCHED !

Written by Daniel Robert Hoy
on 02/17/18

FOCALIZING MIDDAY !
BELLS CHIMED !
RESONATING PLATEAU !

Written by Daniel Robert Hoy
on 02/18/18

REFRESHING MINDS !
AFTERNOON NAPPING !
CULTIVATING INTELLIGENCE !

Written by Daniel Robert Hoy
on 02/19/18

NORMAL LIVING !
ACCEPTED STANDARD !
WAGING COMFORT !

Written by Daniel Robert Hoy
on 02/20/18

TAXING BENEFIT !
OFFICE EXERCISING !
FITTING PROGRAM !

Written by Daniel Robert Hoy
on 02/21/18

HUMANS CAPTURING !
ARRESTING HUMANOIDS !
CONTROLS RECYCLED !

Written by Daniel Robert Hoy
on 02/10/18

ZEUS CLONED !
DRONES CELEBRATING !
COERCING SUPERIORS !

Written by Daniel Robert Hoy
on 02/11/18

CELEBRATING CIRCUS !
WHALES SMOKING !
LIONS DRINKING !

Written by Daniel Robert Hoy
on 02/12/18

TUNNELING UNDERGROUND !
VENTILATION EXHAUSTING !
MINERS SIGHED !

Written by Daniel Robert Hoy
on 02/22/18

PROTECTING PRESS !
CENSORSHIP ABOLISHED !
SPEAKING FREELY !

Written by Daniel Robert Hoy
on 02/23/18

INSURANCE REQUIRED !
RISKY MISDOING !
BALANCING CURE !

Written by Daniel Robert Hoy
on 02/24/18

UNITED PLEDGE !
FREEDOM PROTECTED !
ALLEGING HERETOFORE !

Written by Daniel Robert Hoy
on 02/25/18

COURTING CRIME !
JUVENILE DEFENDED !
PARENTING CODES !

Written by Daniel Robert Hoy
on 02/26/18

PRODUCTS IMPORTED !
POISONING CHILDREN !
ORIGINS UNKNOWN !

Written by Daniel Robert Hoy
on 02/27/18

GROWING THIRST !
SEED PLANTED !
ENRICHING SOIL !

Written by Daniel Robert Hoy
on 02/28/18

SEEING OPPORTUNITIES !
GENERATIONS CREATING !
IMPROVED UNEMPLOYMENT !

Written by Daniel Robert Hoy
on 03/01/18

STROLLING MOONWALKER !
CITY DREAMING !
FEELING SAFE !

Written by Daniel Robert Hoy
on 03/02/18

SHARING KNOWLEDGE !
EDUCATION AVAILABLE !
LIMITING NOBODY !

Written by Daniel Robert Hoy
on 03/03/18

FLOWING AQUIFERS !
NATURALLY SAFEGUARDING !
REFRESHING WATERS !

Written by Daniel Robert Hoy
on 03/04/18

POPULACE CHALLENGING !
EYEBALLING GOVERNMENT !
TRANSPARENCY LEGISLATED !

Written by Daniel Robert Hoy
on 03/05/18

IMPERSONAL WORSHIPING !
EMPOWERING SPIRITUALITY !
RELIGIONS CONFLICTED !

Written by Daniel Robert Hoy
on 03/06/18

NEEDS REQUIRED !
REMOVING POVERTY !
WANTING MORE !

Written by Daniel Robert Hoy
on 03/07/18

SCANDINAVIANS DOGSLEDDING !
MUSHING HUSKIES !
PAWING SNOW !

Written by Daniel Robert Hoy
on 03/08/18

GALAPAGOS ORIGINATING !
ANCHORING DARWIN !
TORTOISES ENDURED !

Written by Daniel Robert Hoy
on 03/09/18

KIWIS RUNNING !
CLIMBING ZEALANDIA !
DANCING HAKA !

Written by Daniel Robert Hoy
on 03/10/18

DOMESTICATING HORSES !
MONGOLIANS MOUNTING !
TENDING HERDS !

Written by Daniel Robert Hoy
on 03/11/18

VOLCANOES ERUPTED !
AEOLIANS ISLANDING !
MYTHICAL BEGINNING !

Written by Daniel Robert Hoy
on 03/12/18

WANDERING PARIS !
ART ENDOWED !
WELCOMING BLISS !

Written by Daniel Robert Hoy
on 03/13/18

BUSH WALKING !
ANIMALS APPROACHING !
AWAKENING AFRICA !

Written by Daniel Robert Hoy
on 03/14/18

ICEBERG BEACHED !
EARTHSHAKING BLACKOUT !
ICELAND STEAMING !
Written by Daniel Robert Hoy
on 03/15/18

HOPPING KANGAROOS !
KOALAS EATING !
POUCHED AUSTRALIANS !
Written by Daniel Robert Hoy
on 03/16/18

SCOTLAND KILTED !
TOSSING CABERS !
BAGPIPES PLAYING !
Written by Daniel Robert Hoy
on 03/17/18

WINDING CANALS !
GONDOLIER ROWING !
ROMANCING VENICE !
Written by Daniel Robert Hoy
on 03/18/18

REDWOODS ELEVATED !
STRETCHING CALIFORNIA !
UPLIFTING RELICS !
Written by Daniel Robert Hoy
on 03/19/18

JUMPING FJORDS !
VIKINGS BURNING !
SAILING BEYOND !
Written by Daniel Robert Hoy
on 03/20/18

UNITED PLEDGE !
FREEDOM PROTECTED !
ALLEGING HERETOFORE !
Written by Daniel Robert Hoy
on 02/25/18

COURTING CRIME !
JUVENILE DEFENDED !
PARENTING CODES !
Written by Daniel Robert Hoy
on 02/26/18

PRODUCTS IMPORTED !
POISONING CHILDREN !
ORIGINS UNKNOWN !
Written by Daniel Robert Hoy
on 02/27/18

BALI FLOODING !
TERRACED RICE !
DEITIES TEMPLED !
Written by Daniel Robert Hoy
on 03/21/18

SURFING PORTUGAL !
AZORES POINTING !
DISCOVERING PLATEAU !
Written by Daniel Robert Hoy
on 03/22/18

SARAJEVO TUNNELED !
BEACHED NEUM !
BOSNIA CONNECTED !
Written by Daniel Robert Hoy
on 03/23/18

AUSTRIA DREAMING !
CLIMBING ALPINES !
VIENNA SINGING !
Written by Daniel Robert Hoy
on 03/24/18

GHANA RAINING !
ABOUNDING VOLTA !
ACCRA INVIGORATED !
Written by Daniel Robert Hoy
on 03/25/18

VIETNAM DRUMMING !
BALANCED CUISINE !
ANCESTORS TASTING !
Written by Daniel Robert Hoy
on 03/26/18

MARACAIBO OVERFLOWING !
BEAUTIFYING VENEZUELA !
CARACAS ELEVATED !
Written by Daniel Robert Hoy
on 03/27/18

ALLURING CAMELS !
DESERT LANDSCAPED !
RIFTING ARABIA !
Written by Daniel Robert Hoy
on 03/28/18

LVIV DRINKING !
BALANCING UKRAINE !
KIEV BARTERED !
Written by Daniel Robert Hoy
on 03/29/18

VOLCAN ERUPTING !
GUATEMALANS PATTERNED !
TASTING AVOCADOS !
Written by Daniel Robert Hoy
on 03/30/18

CHEESEMAKING SWISS !
POLYGLOTS YODELED !
PEACEKEEPING WATCHMAKER !
Written by Daniel Robert Hoy
on 03/31/18

RELAXING YOGA !
MONSOONS BREATHING !
POPULATING INDIA !
Written by Daniel Robert Hoy
on 04/01/18

DIVING REEFS !
EXPLORING BELIZE !
JAGUARS SLEEPING !
Written by Daniel Robert Hoy
on 04/02/18

BAOBABS ANIMATED !
FRAMING MADAGASCAR !
LEMURS ISOLATED !
Written by Daniel Robert Hoy
on 04/03/18

CLIMBING FUJI !
JAPAN BLOSSOMING !
SHRINING PHENOMENA !
Written by Daniel Robert Hoy
on 04/04/18

FENNECS EAVESDROPPING !
COURTING ALGERIA !
SAHARA DOMINATING !

Written by Daniel Robert Hoy
on 04/05/18

PENGUINS COLONIZED !
STRETCHING CHILE !
OVERLOOKING ANDES !

Written by Daniel Robert Hoy
on 04/06/18

LATIUM ROMANCING !
ITALIANS CELEBRATING !
BULLYING WOLF !

Written by Daniel Robert Hoy
on 04/07/18

WALLED PANDAS !
COMPASSING CHINA !
PRINTING TEALEAVES !

Written by Daniel Robert Hoy
on 04/08/18

LUANDA PROMENADING !
MASKING ANGOLA !
CABINDA SURROUNDED !

Written by Daniel Robert Hoy
on 04/09/18

MEXICO COMMEMORATING !
TRAVELING MONARCHS !
SNORKELING YUCATAN !

Written by Daniel Robert Hoy
on 04/10/18

GERMANY COMPOSING !
INNOVATING MUNICH !
DINKELSBUHL CHARMED !

Written by Daniel Robert Hoy
on 04/11/18

CHARMING CAMBODIA !
ANGKOR DEVOTED !
TREKKING CARDAMOM !

Written by Daniel Robert Hoy
on 04/12/18

RAINING MANAUS !
CURITIBA PLANNING !
FLOURISHED BRAZIL !

Written by Daniel Robert Hoy
on 04/13/18

NAVIGATING OKAVANGO !
KALAHARI THIRSTING !
CANOEING BOTSWANA !

Written by Daniel Robert Hoy
on 04/14/18

JUTLAND OVERSEEING !
TRICKING ZEALAND !
DENMARK ARTICULATING !

Written by Daniel Robert Hoy
on 04/15/18

ENCHANTING PHILIPPINES !
ISLANDS HOPPING !
RIPPLING CAVES !

Written by Daniel Robert Hoy
on 04/16/18

JAGGED BASQUES !
EBRO NAMING !
SPANIARDS BULLFIGHTING !

Written by Daniel Robert Hoy
on 04/17/18

NILE FLOWING !
BUILDING EGYPT !
GIZA REIGNED !

Written by Daniel Robert Hoy
on 04/18/18

AMASSED CASTLES !
VRŠATEC PEAKING !
CROWNING SLOVAKIA !

Written by Daniel Robert Hoy
on 04/19/18

UNITING SLAVS !
RUSSIA SPANNING !
CULTIVATING BALLET !

Written by Daniel Robert Hoy
on 04/20/18

DANCING STILTS !
WILDEBEESTS MIGRATING !
BEHOLDING KENYA !

Written by Daniel Robert Hoy
on 04/21/18

HUASCARÁN AVALANCHING !
SACSAYHUAMÁN STONEWALLED !
SURFING PERUVIANS !

Written by Daniel Robert Hoy
on 04/22/18

INDULGING PUBS !
TENORS DANCING !
IRELAND BEAUTIFIED !

Written by Daniel Robert Hoy
on 04/23/18

TANGIER MANEUVERING !
MARRAKESH TRADING !
TREKKING MOROCCO !

Written by Daniel Robert Hoy
on 04/24/18

PAGODAS GILDED !
BALLOONING BAGAN !
MYANMAR FLOATING !

Written by Daniel Robert Hoy
on 04/25/18

MOOSE CANOEING !
STARGAZING CANADA !
BELUGAS SMILING !

Written by Daniel Robert Hoy
on 04/26/18

WINDMILLS DRAINING !
PAINTING CANALS !
NETHERLANDS BLOOMING !

Written by Daniel Robert Hoy
on 04/27/18

GORILLAS MOUNTAINEERING !
THUNDERING CONGO !
OKAPIS ROAMING !

Written by Daniel Robert Hoy
on 04/28/18

FENNECS EAVESDROPPING !
COURTING ALGERIA !
SAHARA DOMINATING !

Written by Daniel Robert Hoy
on 04/05/18

PENGUINS COLONIZED !
STRETCHING CHILE !
OVERLOOKING ANDES !

Written by Daniel Robert Hoy
on 04/06/18

LATIUM ROMANCING !
ITALIANS CELEBRATING !
BULLYING WOLF !

Written by Daniel Robert Hoy
on 04/07/18

ARGENTINA TANGOING !
SLICING IGUAZA !
GLACIERS ADVANCING !

Written by Daniel Robert Hoy
on 04/29/18

ENRICHED VISTULA !
WISENTS ROAMING !
POLAND UNSPOILED !

Written by Daniel Robert Hoy
on 04/30/18

HIGHLANDS REIGNING !
REGIMENTED ROYALTY !
SCOTLAND CROWNED !

Written by Daniel Robert Hoy
on 05/01/18

DESCENDING LALIBELA !
AXUM RISING !
PLATEAUING ETHIOPIA !

Written by Daniel Robert Hoy
on 05/02/18

MISSISSIPPI OVERWHELMING !
BREATHTAKING YOSEMITE !
AMERICA DAYDREAMING !

Written by Daniel Robert Hoy
on 05/03/18